from heartbreak to hopeful

SHELBY CATALANO

Dedication:

*To anyone who's ever been robbed of joy
from heartbreak.
May you rediscover hopefulness
within these pages.*

A note from the author

I've had this idea since 2015 – and it's safe to say a lot has changed. What's in your hands now is a collection of poems I've created over years based on my own loves, losses, hurts, and the journey for the most important thing of all: self love. Since heartbreak and hope are two ends of a great divide, I was inspired to weave in an overarching narrative with these poems that lets anyone find the stage of their heart they felt strongest. You can read this book backwards or forward, as these pieces together are designed to fit the narrative chronologically. Feeling extra gleeful? Go back first. In limbo with how you should feel after a breakup? The middle has your perfect dose of melancholy.

This collection is meant to be messy and unapologetic. There's differing techniques, art styles, and inner darknesses I explored. But I wouldn't want anything else to be my first self-published work.

I hope you find solace in these words and peace that you can be you – whatever your flower looks like at the moment.

Xoxo,
Shelby

From Heartbreak to Hopeful
A dual-sided poetry collection about rediscovering self love

print ISBN: 978-1-66782-373-7
ebook ISBN: 978-1-66782-374-4

Contents

MIDDLE

HOPE

HEARTBREAK

THE END - OR THE BEGINNING?

Is this the end or the beginning?
It's up to you –

The end of one thing
Often leads to something new
A place more... true
To dull our heartache

Stare out the window
Burn the picture frame
Feel the warmth
But feel nothing really

The lines on the road stretch on
Painted arrows, beckoning
Perhaps..   calling
for the start of a new chapter

One person's end is another's beginning
So turn these pages differently
In order to retrace your steps
And remember who you are

at every stage of heartbreak
and hope

Water your flowers
And watch them start to bloom
This is over
Now you have room

To set roots somewhere new
and more true

You'll never know
Unless you travel back
Forward
And back again

Wherever your heart takes you then
You'll know...   it's still you

IT'S OVER

No death hurts as bad
As the death of true, true love
Woven into harp strings
Hundreds of chords sounding
Turning fingers bloody
All of it stripped away to dust

He left me
Dried blood caked in my brain
About many things
Did he just give up?
Loosen the strings until there was no choice but to
cut them up?

The hurt hangs around me like miasma
Slashing my breath
Lungs become chopped
Blood pooling in my mouth

As an asexual woman
Feeling rejection on the highest level
For being me
Made the strings feel extra sharp
As my fingers plucked the loosened strings

I am diced
I am clouded with an impossible hurt
That demands to be played
A refrain
That only my deafened ears will hear on repeat

It's over it's over it's over
How could this happen?

A TASTE OF TORMENT

A fragment of flavor
Sweet, rotting tooth –
Embolden my senses
And leave me aloof

Bite my lip
And taste test poison
A tiny portion
Lost devotion

Shackle my legs
Leave me lonely
Torturing me
My one and only

Death of companion
Losing restraint
Inhibitions gone
This is true torment

FROM LOVER TO OVER

It only takes one letter
To go from a lover to over
Being over it – and over you
To becoming something entirely different –
An *other*

OUTCAST

When depression lingers
The weight on your chest so heavy
and laden with no sign of rest
When you feel like no matter what you do
Your inclusion is temporary
Feeling in the outer rim of a universe
That never wanted you
Or asked you to belong

What can you do when you feel like an outcast
The pain will always last
Hurt hurt hurt
Till your chest caves in
Then you get worse worse worse
And the pain sets in

When you feel like an observer
In a group of all your friends
You can't help being lonely
Will this feeling ever end?
Bereft of priority, of being #1
You'll always be second
In a crowd of someones

What does it mean to actually be wanted?
Why am I alone in a group of all my loved ones
Unhappy; unfulfilled, and utterly depressed
Staring straight ahead
But my mind's across the world
     In orbit

Outcast, outcast
Don't make it last
Don't want to be an
Outcast, outcast – anymore

Tendrils of feeling grip my gut and make me nauseous
Friendship after friendship burns
Makin' me feel cautious
To trust
To love
To start again
This is the end

What will make me feel like anything but an
    Outcast

I guess some things just... last
forever.

RED ROSES

It had to be red roses
It was your last piece of flint
Its flying embers climax
In a single tiny glint

Curtain call, the thorns hit me
Troves of flowers bound and bit she
Your friendly gesture a selfish plea
Bloody petals avoid being free

Release enchantment
A fool's errand
Intensified by the resentment
of comparing

Red shades of binding
A shorter wavelength
Warm toned reminding
your sneaky play at strength

Take them away, foul buds
Your smell won't lure me in
Rejecting color blood
is the simplest way to say "fin."

ICE CREAM SCOOP

Scooped clean
No more left
The space between
Feels cramped yet   exposed   and   spacious
Galaxy of innards' graves
I crave nothing
No hunger to mention

Emotionally I'm all dried up
So scoop it out
And leave none left
The nerve endings are deadened too
No capacity left
To feel you too

No joy no pain, take another scoop
I feel nothing
Yet weight feels drooped
A thousand pounds of emptiness
Is far, far worse than stones or death

You can take it all away too
Simply grab the handle
It's time to scoop!

I'VE GOT TO BE THE CRAZY ONE

Your scathing words cut
through my hand
Blood dripping down my palm
Here we go again

I could not see your dark intent
The liquid slipping through
I thought I knew what you could do
But then I saw anew

A fence put up, you tear it down
You want inside my house
The front door locked and painted black
An entrance unannounced

I did not want you in my home
You did not want to leave
The pots and pans were banging then
I had not one reprieve

At first I thought that this was fine
That men get what they want
Until I grabbed the pot handle
And swung on all your taunts

You gaslighter, I heard you say
You twisted all my kindness
But my home was the broken one
Accosted by my blindness

I locked you out, I tried I tried
A padlock with a key
While heartbreak whooshed in wanton light
Familiar songs to me

The tune went on its merry way
Shutters slapped my space
Ill-fitted fiends bent from the spots
All thoughts, all out of place

Am I the evil wrongdoer?
Should I be slain today?
For why else would you deface
The truths I have to say?

My hands flash with a sharpening
My teeth are soaked with blood
The villain that I want to see
Just simply turns to mud

I cannot demonize myself
For saying what I feel
And I refuse to succumb
To what isn't real

ALL CLAWS AND NO CLASS

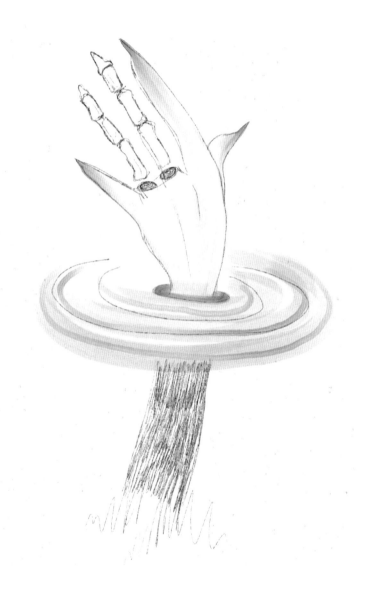

All claws and no class
Makes for a very bitey woman
A drifty druid

Malevolence clinging to pores
Traveling dew on an early morning flower
Droplets scattering with all the fervor
of spilled sugar

Her drooping eyes feel heavy
With oppression
An underlying obsession
Stop the lesion;
a pause, a cacophony
of fog
Turned to smog
Filtered breathing;
the AC of sleepless nights

Her eyelids further closing out the toxicity
The door of dreams shut
No more air
No more mist
No more space to breathe
But she is safe

As she digs her roots in, splintering nails made of bark
The last song of the lark
She recedes into the dark
No longer a danger
Only a ranger

To what dreams and nightmares may come
From herself, and no one else

SCHADENFREUDE

There's a sick satisfaction in knowing
Someone who caused you pain is suffering too
But that pleasure quickly turns sour
A foul karmic reminder
That misdeeds can harbor

FEAR

A fresh serving of fear
Blankets our eyes in wool
To become an unthinking tool
For reaching into the unknown

My fear branches out
Yet the twigs on me snap
Leaves falling
Autumn finishing the trap

Fear is the death of curiosity
When we lose a questioning touch
We are often walking dead ourselves

Panic panic catastrophe
What'll it be
next

When fear runs your life
Your life runs on fear

BITTER

A taste
And a feeling
Of a place
Not of healing

Folding chest
Into unrest
Forced arrest
A hateful nest

Push it down push it down
To drown
Straight into our crown
Vocals never found

BATTLING WITH AMBITION

If you want to curse your children
Curse them to always be ambitious
For ambition is never sated;
It's an ever-growing, unquenchable thirst;
It lingers long after the endorphins of achievement
fade away;
It always seeks more, like an eternal glutton.

Nothing can best ambition, for it never sleeps
It's doomed to continue long after the Nobel prize
or certificate is complete,
For the next step is always in front of you,
and you're doomed to keep trying
for the sheer fact that the step is in front of you.
You put it there, yet you can't stop flying.
You're
         consumed by it.
Ambition put it there.

Everyone tells you to aim for the sky, but
look what that did to Icarus.

I'm crying, yet no one hears you cry in space.
I'm in my own vacuum of ambition
I am my own Sisyphus, where my boulder is success
And my mountain constantly changing.
First my boulder was high school;
then college, and then
get a nice job that fulfills me,

for surely then I would be successful and content.
But then contentment and complacency
capture me at the crest
and I find myself at the bottom of the hill
Once again
Of unrest

I'm bested by my own ambition, and enslaved to its shove
to always aim higher, and
be a better version of myself;
whatever the hell that means.

So if you ever wish to curse someone
with the deepest lashings of malcontent,
look no further than ambition's talons
to dig into their chest.

I've found no greater pain than my own mind
refusing to be happy
simply because of the fiery ambition
that burns in my core
and never stops.
You could say...
I'm
      consumed by it.

MAJOR DEPRESSIVE DISORDER

When I'm on top of the world
I look over the edge... and know
That eventually I'll find my way back
To the place I deplore most...
The bottom

It's inevitable. A resounding circle
Of major depressive disorder
That can make functioning
at a sustainable level
Difficult
and sometimes impossible.
It usually starts like this:
I'm on top of the cliff
killing it;
I never want this euphoric feeling to end
... But I know it will
Yet I still seize the moment with a fire and a grace
That's unparalleled in a human moment.

And yet.

There I am – face to face with the reflection in the water.
The edge.
The   precipice.
It mocks me; rippling, tiny rocks falling off the edge.
You'll be joining soon enough, it whispers.
You always come back to me.

This pull of gravity that forces me down –
Sometimes slowly, sometimes quicker than I can grasp
And then I'm submerged,
Drowning, dissociating again,
That vague, robotic functioning,
I'm unfortunately accustomed to doing in order to
Make it through the day.

All concepts of control melt away
Under the tempest of the waves
As I know fighting is futile.
It's never been about control – just *survival*.
Just knowing I can brace myself for the pressure
the water to seal me in
For the next bout of unplugged reality
Where I'm struggling to find the power
To move, or put on a happy face
Past the bubbles coming out of my mouth, where I'm
Out of air. Out of time.
But no worries, I think
As the bubbles billow in front of me
My lifesource
Yet I don't move, because I've got no fight left; only despair
...   for a time.

And yet.

Like every other instance,
I'll eventually find my way back to the surface again,
The buoyancy of my mood fluctuating once more
After battle with my mind has made me weary
Albeit with bruised ribs, bloody knuckles, and tears
But I can claim that victory; I earned it.
Air is mine again – for now.
I broke free once more
From that underwater prison
That envelops me from time to time.

I climb the cliff
To get that feeling once more
Of euphoria
Before it's taken away again
A mental Sisyphus – seeking relief.
Love.
Help.

Keep fighting to find the cliff again
For without a cliff
What are we
But marooned in a watery prison
of our own making?

YOUR LIGHT IS DIMMING

The idea of a different life is quite striking
Shiny even
Thinking you can be someone else
Or another identity entirely
Is almost too irresistible
But many of us romanticize this
Thinking being another person will be
the ointment to every ailment

Destiny is so alluring
We wait for the call, a beckoning from the waters
Or even a summons from another dimension entirely

Most of us won't ever get that call
But the temptation of hearing it...
Even once
Is very, *very* alluring

So I'll keep listening to the waves, hoping
A siren will come out from under it to summon me
And bid me under

LOSING PIECES OF MYSELF

Puzzle pieces splayed
Upon my shelf
I ask myself
How they spread
Unnoticed

That one is ambition
This one self respect
Another a past musician
Here depression unchecked

My corner piece of compassion
Gone and frayed apart
A measly little ration
The horse before the cart

It's lost from thoughts strayed
A mind for someone else
Its simple, lilting playthrough
The corner pieces dealt

You let them slip away, my dear
The pieces that are you
And when you find a clarity – clear
The jigsaw leads to you

Remember what has slipped from you
Gather every piece
For there is nothing you truly lose
That you don't choose to release

ALONE AND LONELY

Alone and lonely
Looking at compassion like outdated fashion
What's free-flowing to some, yet unknowing to me
Eyes like a screen, blurry and unfocused

When vigor's your very trigger
And sensitivity pains every sensation
How do intimacy's silken sheets explain
Your self-inflicted, abusive location

A two-sided mirror I've painted
Its sheen a reminder of every destiny forsook
Crumbs of trust; fallen bread spreading out
Straightforward as a quiz with a textbook

Yet why is intimacy so hard?

Don't touch me
What's it like – don't yearn for something you'll never earn
All you got was ignored and repelled
Why won't you ever learn?

IT'S BEEN 24 HOURS

It's been 24 hours
Since you were home
You're comforting someone else
As I'm alone

Scrubbing dishes
Eyes wet dinner plates
Feeling anger inflate
As I hear you come home late

You return to broken glass
Chest bursting as I cry
You're clueless
"It was fine yesterday," you try

Might I say a lesson on consent –
You can be okay with something one moment
And not the next

The shards are too small
Feelings hidden once more
Your fear of commitment
Made the cracks imminent

It's been 24 hours
Since you came home
You're texting someone else
And I'm...   still alone

KNIFE POINT

I remember the first time you
    Belittled me
Your voice low
Knife drawn
Chopping vegetables
Gruffness as I heard you say
"I'll handle it, move."

My body went numb
I floated to the bedroom
An outsider to my limbs
Back against the bed as I
Slumped down

My hardwiring was awry
Haywire as adrenaline
Hit my blood like a cold gust
I could feel the vibrato in my head
Continue its tinny
Tinnitus
    The pain inflamed

I remember this so clearly
The first memory that something was wrong
That you weren't quite
The person I thought you were

And for what?

I wasn't chopping fast enough for you, was I?
What else wasn't enough for you?

And so the trust chopped to pieces

Can I become a raincloud
So when I cry
It'll be romantically dreary
Instead of the weariness
I'm currently feeling

DENYING SOMETHING'S WRONG

In a head-run society
We ignore our hearts
Becoming a cog
In someone else's parts

In someone else's business
A means to an end
Versus our own means and journey

We are sick
We have been stripped like paint on a wall
To be replaced with parts that aren't ours
That don't feel right
That hurt us

It feels unnatural
But we go on
Hoping the same result will be different tomorrow
That ignoring our purpose will somehow cure
On its own

Something is wrong
Very, very wrong
We have forgotten nature's call
And the plea in our brains
To stop
And smell the smell of our talents and
The perfume of our dreams

Face your inner child and tell them
They are incapable of great things

If you can do that –
Then you've truly given up on yourself.

THE SEASON IS OVER

Because love's so fickle
We desire its thistle
A rare leafy plant
Designed to enchant

Lips round as dew drops
Tickling fringe copse
A whisper so tender
Air rife with its splendor

Passion's exhalation
As you embrace me
My forest's affection
Bloomed every direction

Toes in the soil
Fingers link and coil
A breathy release
As we desire peace

Fondness is soft
A swaying leaf aloft
Until the next season
When fickle turns treason

MIDDLE

Reading from front to back.

FORGIVING YOURSELF: It's not your fault. Take responsibility for your own happiness now. Forgive past You and past Them.

There's something so unceremonious about moving on
One day suddenly just becomes another
And they all blend together into
A blurred memory that becomes the rest of your life

BLAMING YOURSELF: It's all your fault. It's all my fault? My fault...

Reading from back to front

MALADY

Malady
The tune sickly;
Its tempo quickens;
Malady –
My lady –
Women seen as affliction
That must have restrictions

Dress this way
Hold your tongue
You are weak
Come here and play

Your sickness all sin
Dripping in moonblood
Tainted and ill
Rotten within

We cannot win

I THINK BACK HOW I TRUSTED YOU

I think back how I trusted you
Believed in what you said
Our time a foggy piece of mind
That I glimpse in my head

I gaze into the looking glass
Past cracks are staring back
My journey steps me in your arms
A member of your pack

Days blur together dreamily
The happiest of times
But then came all your treachery
My cheerfulness a crime

You took all that I had from me
My song at every verse
A rest that warped all of my shame
Infinitum, a curse

My body vesseled for your truth
Lid tight for every measure
But your love wasn't watertight
The crack was you, a lecher

Your curse infected me anew
The roses of my youth
From all the colors, green to brown
You siphoned out my truth

The final stop was trickery
Curdling all my kindness
Too frail to see the wicked grime
Showing all your blindness

The carriage of my thoughts abrupt
As I leave this behind
A distant mirror of time
Never again to find

YOU WANT ME BACK (I WANT YOU GONE)

You wish I'd put a spell on you
A potion to return
The storybook end far gone
As you slowly come to terms

Sorry, sorry, you want to say
I know I hurt you bad
You want your guilt to go away
A balm to cure your sad

How hard it must be! You wish I'd say
As I embrace you in forgiveness
Your messages and telltale lips
A solution fueling hopefulness

I'll never come back to you – a fact
Not a chant or incantation
Your loneliness your recompense
And repeated stagnation

Losing me a consequence
Of every abusive maneuver
Not any deity or power
Will expunge you, wrongdoer

Never will I smile at your notes
Or awaken you in lust
My garden grows in your absence
Our bond reduced to rust

A BOX OF THOUGHTS

A box of thoughts:

Shake it, hear the gizmos clink
No, not the familiar car honking bit
A wind chime tinkles in a blink
Dirty laundry pushing me past the brink

Kissing eyelashes, vanilla scents
Lacing hands after laughing commenced
Magic bands for recompense
These feelings just won't relent

Comforting you after a loved one died
Rubbing back circles as you cried
Waves crashed, with nowhere to hide
Nothing left but submit to the tide

Once a mess, now in pieces
No more rent on these mental leases
The wrinkles already made their creases
The bitter taste after the sweetness

Back under the bed it goes
Desperate to be erased
Destined to be remembered

LIKE WATER

Tides recede
And so do feelings
Lapping our ankles
And wanting us freely

Dance in the waves
As the moon waxes full
Waves upon waves
As the next feeling dulls

Splashing the sand
Moonbeams faded
Your memory crashing
And leaving me jaded

TRIMMING

Chop the hair
Buy new clothes
Everyone knows
A woman needs to go –

And evolve herself.

A sinew for her heartbreak
Cut this follicle; use its string
A new thread by which
To reinvent –

And fully start again.

Cast this hair into the depths
Banish its power
It clings to what was
And has now gone away –

No more pain.

A ritual cleansing
New color, new angles
Perspective is changing
An emotional equation –

A new day for growth.

WINDOW SHOPPING

Why am I shopping
In front of browser windows
Tabs and tabs
Searching
Indexing
Scrolling
For what I have no ability to open

When will that person come?
A pretty dress with frills
Or a dark lined vest?
Look
There's a risk-free 90 day trial here
Heartbreak will happen
Hope fleeting
Feeling lost on the dark web
Caught in its tangles
Viscous webbing on my fingers
Channeling through the internet
Dirtying my hands
Soon they are thick cocoons
Each finger trapped
Thumping the keyboard
What am I even searching for?
Scroll, scroll, scroll
Don't think
Click, click

But it comes anyway
You're alone you're alone you're alone

Time to open another tab!
The search starts again
For what...
      I'm still trying to figure out

EMPTINESS

You wait for the kiss
An imagined wire taut
Pulling at tension in the air
You can feel the cut of the string
This entropy grating your nerves
With antici...
    But the "pation" never comes

A FLYING ABNORMALITY

My abnormality skims
The skyline
A brave attempt
At graceful limbs
Every day a question –
A direction
How shall I fly?
My next course correct
Feebly chosen
Like a pierced wing
To live like myself
Or like my other kin
Passing for fear of
Isolation, or a false
Identity
Drafts pick me up
Tumbling through
The current, begging
Yet I cannot fly true
A maelstrom against all reason
Not my season
You feel it too –
The winds of change
Except I'm my own compass
And point of view
Flying to the horizon of dusk
Emboldened by my blood-thirsty fangs
For I'm not a bird
But a vampire
How come you never knew?

DON'T LET MY PAST DICTATE MY PRESENT

Don't let yesterday control me today

Past it all –
Lemons sour tears my precedent
Suck in my cheeks
exhale
and glower my reticence
The shame of my benevolence

Face the present –
Suppressive waves tingle at my throat
Claw at my face
inhale
and stay afloat
The panic subsides every note

Embrace the future –
Beauty ripples my stinging tears
Shut my eyes
breathe
and melt away the years
The dissolution of my fears

From now on
        I live every day for me

HOPE

CLIFFSIDE

I wait by the cliff
On the craggy bumps of my elbow and forearm
Resting. Digesting.
The spindly branches of a tree
Fingers light as spores
On the cliff face of my chin.

The lines curve around
The bark on my phalanges
Aged. Frayed.
Too many rings to count
The redwood of my inner thoughts

Every day a new root to discover
A new tree to uncover
As a frail leaf
Comes out of the ground
A thought
Demanding to be felt
And seen
A light beneath
The wind of new ideas
A new thought begins.

DO YOU BELIEVE?

Do you believe in the red string of fate
Whose tethers tie you to what you create?
Such fragile conception; what blithe repose
To have your life laid out right beneath your nose

Does it scare you to know that your life is one string
That's tied to everything that was, has, will bring
Such fear in your eyes; bated breath that you hold
To know this is the autonomy you've sold

Does it hurt you to be connected to one person
Who lights up your world, yet the risks of it worsen
Such overthinking; what pain in your chest
To face losing the thing you love best

Whether a red string of fate, or the choices you make
Never lose sight of the things you create

GROOMED

Cracked perception – interjection
Your lips crashed into mine
it then gave way to infection
That left me there, to pine

I was told to keep it secret
As you led me back to crowds
Hand in mine, rising pleasure
The darkness blinding sounds

My youth felt electricity
In lieu of stinging zaps
The burn marks of complicity
Where I failed to feel the gaps

Your tongue plated in silver
Lip glints with shiny metal
Heavy spoken slithers
A soft tinny, yet all nettles

False promises shrunk me; I felt so small
I trusted you implicitly
Yet here, aloof, I crawl
A mere pawn of your bigotry

Withered as I left my water
In place to drink your poison
Yet never did I falter
Until the facade began an oil spill

Down the perfect castle went
Your gnarly hands backfiring
The deception withdrawing; heaven sent
As I rerouted my wiring

The forest floor felt damp and weary
As I wandered through alone
No matter that I was needy
I reaped what had been sown

I thought your actions were my fault
Wasted years on all the shame
When I realized it was a result
Of grooming that was to blame

On and on, I clawed the ground
Searching for the answers
The wet dirt came to a mound
As I removed the bloating cancers

My heartbeat veins of groundwater
Took a breath from all the sourness
A hole remained; your deepest plotter
Testaments to the foulness

Twisted like a dishtowel
Strewn words my field of flowers
All beaten and gutted bowels
Forgotten were the hours

Now you avert your eyes under a cap
A shadow whispering shame
But once you peel it back, a zap!
Electricity gone as it came

The sun choreographs in my chest
Formidable fuertes all the same
They twirl a sadness on my breast
The last pas de chat of shame

A galaxy of emotions send nebulas in my eyes
Glittering; full of possibilities
For I survived, and I rise
Instead of your control and fragilities

Twists and taciturn moments remain
Yet I'm here to claim my voice back
My very last refrain
My life – my success – your payback

DECEMBER NIGHTS

The joy of
a cold, December night
Twinkling lights
Talking about children
a spark of your future

gone out –
never meant for me.

AWAKENING

You're one decision away from awakening
Aspiration into affirmation
Quieting the derision
In your heart.

Open eyes mean an open heart
Unfurling for fortuitous greeting
In solid heartbeating
Freeing.

Wake up, wake up!
Your alarm clock is ringing.
Why do you wait
To turn off its repeating?

HOW TO BE YOURSELF AGAIN

At the end of it all you'll only have yourself
In pieces and in health
And all you can do is take the pieces
For how to be yourself

Take that shard of abuse
Twist it in your gut
feel it refuse –
        to give in
It bends, but does not break,
Because such memories often take
Much longer to abate

But shards of glass, when put together
Make a beautiful mosaic of color and splendor
That memory, this feeling, your tightly clenched fist
All add up to you – so assert you exist

You're the only You there ever will be
So smile because it happened
Not because you're who you want to see
Yet in that mirror of glass
That refracts all your faults
The person that seems less like you
Is learning from self assault

The glass pushed together makes one large mosaic
Shifting unquestions; even more complications

A breakup is just one shard of glass
In many you'll have in years to pass

So remember the next time another piece breaks
That you are the person you choose to create

RE-LEARNING WHO YOU ARE

A breakup is like a crime scene
Where the breath between life and death
Make all the difference in the world

Your chalk outline stares back at you
On the concrete
An obsolete canvas of your former self

How did this happen?

You laid on the floor, gave them the chalk, and said "Draw"

The blood of your identity spattered
On the walls for all to see your sacrifice

Giving up yourself
Meant you gave your life to another
When it should be mutual
As lovers

Diagnose the scene
Play detective
Find the evidence
It doesn't make sense

Take it back
Justice for yourself
In micro affirmations
And adulation

You'll cleanse this space
Where no more blood
Will be spilled

KINTSUGI

I'm fluent in fuck-all
And floating in sexuality
I feel the cracks
Chipping away at me

Every splinter
Invites more growth
Banishing the roots of self-limiting beliefs

Less polish, more splendor
For rough around the edges
Is kintsugi

I wish to rebuild
The fractures opening space
For golden goodness
To glow
To go
To grow

Imperfection
Feels perfect
When you acknowledge
Its beauty

KNOW ETERNITY

I think I know eternity
When I look into your eyes
A summer's breeze and lashes squeeze
And I see your love likewise

As present as mountains stand
Existence unforgiving
When I brush your hair back with my hand
I remember life's worth living

Love's inferno turns volcanic
Every smile ignites this passion
This devotion purely organic
An eruption of lava, my veins exploding

One day I know this fire will ease
But my peaks still stand unerring
Whenever you see it on the horizon
You'll know my love's unyielding

Long after I'm gone, my feelings will stay true
Magma solidified to earth
A stronger bond than anything
Time's truth – love's worth

AGENCY OF A WOMAN

As a woman with agency
Give me the aid to see
A place to be
More than femininity
A reason to fly
Free

LOVE IS MUSIC

Wrapped in my blankets
Body tired, but mind rapt attention
Alert to the music notes
You're plucking in my eyelids

Thoughts drift from my vocal chords
Leaping on the bridge of all words
Of music

Every good boy does fine
Flat here, eighth note laid bare
A minuet of mention
Minutely promised with rest
The score unending
As dreams start a new concerto
A crescendo
Of love

SELF CARE ISN'T SELFISH

In a wait wait wait world
Be your own compassion
Wrapped in self love;
Packaged with silence;
Embraced with empathy
for what's happening in your mind

In a wait wait wait world
Find what you need and nurture it:
Plant the seeds of sensitivity;
Water your cheeks, then wipe them away
Knowing you've given yourself the nourishment you need
To grow

And give yourself the mantra:
I am here
I am strong
I trust myself
I trust in my abilities
I am not my productivity
I am worthy of love

Develop a predilection for loving yourself
And you'll see all the beginnings of you
Begin to blossom

A new you
A stronger you
A more compassionate you
The best version of yourself has shown up
And etched love into the stars
A constellation for all

In a wait wait wait world
Take a breath
And hold every moment as a precious stash
To be kind to yourself, and to others
Let the stars gleam, and your smile widen
For this, too, shall pass

SKINCARE ROUTINE

The pinnacle of self love
Lies in treating your skin with deliciousness
Juicy care to spark joy
Using your cleanser says,
"I will keep toxins from you"
As the impurities go down the drain
Using your moisturizer replies,
"Your ongoing health is important to me"
Using your sunscreen declares,
"I will protect you from harm"
Taking time to love every pore
Makes room for more
Love in your life

The ritual invites us to look in the mirror and say
"you're worth love and care."
The minutes of scrubbing away the day
Exfoliating the space we had
To create a new container to court

We are comprised of cycles –
Our skin constantly sheds
In a ring of life and death

When skin meets
Hands caressing our face
a tiny embrace
we make space

For ourselves.

WATERBENDER

The breath in my ears
Is ocean sounds inside a shell
Seafoam in and out –
Like the tide as it sighs
against the sand

In and out

I am water
I am power

I cup my hands and breathe
The shape of a shell
The shape of my birth canal
An oval of possibilities
As the tide – gaping and wide –
Sweeps me inward

PRISM

A lady's like a prism
All shapes and moving splendor
Her smile radiates the rainbow
As her deepened dimples glow

Every body sway a triangle
An angle to be discovered
Seeing her revolve in sunlight
Makes every moment brighter

There's a sharpness to her dancing elbows
A two-step; jagged, yet unknowable
I yearn to see her colors
As yearning turns
"I love her"

YOU'RE THE BONE TO MY BROTH

A hearty marriage is as good as soup
Boiled and brothy, smells galore
Too much salt, but stirred just right,
Ingredients dumped into a pot

You lose track of the cooking temp
Laughing, crying, egg timer set
The stove then simmers, bubbling hot
A marriage in a steamy pot

Once over seasoned, other cups bland
But every lesson learned hand in hand
Your partner sips and smiles again
A bowl of memories only you two share

WHEN YOU'RE ENOUGH FOR SOMEONE

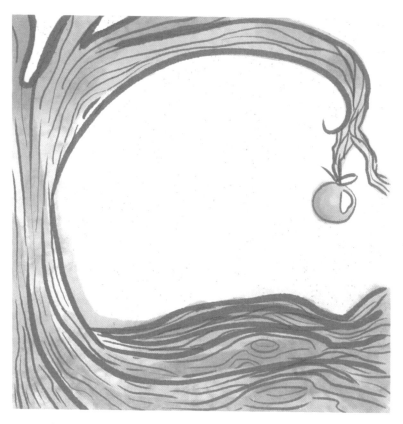

Enough
Fills me to eternity
Knowing my soul
Satisfies yours
Not more – not less
Enough

EUPHORIA

The days blur together,
I want to envision today
I was a demon
Dancing in a circle
Sharp flames curling and billowing in licks of heat
Where I rode the top of the world
And climaxed like I damn well pleased.

This vision of conquering the world
We should all keep in mind
Meddling with monsters beneath us
Crushing them with big thighs
That waxed in popularity – much like bushy eyebrows.

I am the goddess of my fate
Three moons flanking each other
Into a trinity of life
And death.

True, I probably only envisioned this
On Saturday
But any business owner will tell you
Having a vision is the first step
Toward a great goal and purpose.

What's your purpose in this euphoria?
Pray tell me.
Before you go calling
a raven black
as a crow.

MY MIRROR SHIELD

Who I am with you
Shines brighter than ever
You are my mirror shield
Amplifying what was once
A trickle of light
To make a sunny chandelier
Dance beams like glittering baubles
Across the walls
A rising and falling waltz
Of what you do to me
Inside

I feel the dance
Every golden gleam another step
A skip and fluttering beat
As sunlight pours from every corner
And shadows frolic
Against its brilliance

I feel my personality radiant
In your sunlight
A shadow cast
In harsh relief
Myself, yet brighter
A self portrait reflecting back
In your eyes
My mirror shield
How brilliant you shine
And reflect back on me
All the things I wish to be

You are not diminished
But an augmentation
Of everything I am
Feeling the tingles of warmth
Echo magnificence
Around each iris
I am the moon in front of the sun
Eclipsed, yet enhanced by your magnitude
In awe of you
As you get brighter
And I darker
Yet
Together, harmonious,
And everything the couple
Made for each other
I now understand
My darkness does not tarnish
Your multitudes
But enhances how bright you are instead
And knowing this
I am whole
Shadows and all

Special acknowledgements

To my love Dain – thank you for being the person I needed to finish this draft the right way – as a happy ending, and not a tragedy.

My editor, Autumn – thank you for your endless encouragement and presence in my vulnerability to make my writing the best, most authentic version of myself.

To my sister, Steph - grateful for your lifetime of support, camaraderie, and Piscean "all or nothing" honesty. You saw this in its infancy before anyone else and always had my back on it.

To Megan & Judy – ample love for the late nights and unwavering support as I tormented over this on the couch.

To my family – thanks for supporting me, even if I am a bit of a black sheep.

To my readers – thank you for giving this book space in your lives. May it enrich you as much as it healed me to create.

To my editor, Autumn.

About the author

Shelby Catalano is a Pacific Northwest based writer, poet, and general jack of all trades. She's been published in The Raven Review, Poetically Magazine, and the Deviant: Chronicles of Pride anthology from Inkfeathers Publishing. Her debut poetry collection *From Heartbreak to Hopeful* celebrates love and loss in all its forms – no matter where you are in your personal journey. When not writing for freelance clients or being a marketer by day, she enjoys indie video games, used bookstores, and nebulously traveling and practicing chaos magic to ward off existential dread.

Follow the author
Twitter: sherubicat
IG: shelbycatcreates
Website: www.shelbycatalano.com

from

hopeful

to

heartbreak

SHELBY CATALANO

From Heartbreak to Hopeful is a dual-sided poetry collection that follows the path to self love from life-shattering heartbreak. Following romance in all its forms, you'll traverse heartbreak at its lowest point and find the way back to yourself in hope and self love. Inspiring verse, witty affirmations, and nail-biting anticipation, this collection explores gut-wrenching reminders of how heartbreak changes us – and how it ultimately makes us better in the end. Self-illustrated and written, this debut collection normalizes the spectrum of heartbreak and celebrates hope by allowing readers to read backwards and forwards for two complete stories. By finding the state of your heart in these pages, you can begin something new for yourself with the lessons you've learned.